THE CROSS AND THE CRIES OF HUMAN NEED

MESSAGES FOR LENT AND EVERY SEASON

The Meaning of the Cross for Human Problems
Portrayed in Six Selections from the Plays of

Arthur Miller

John Osborne

Edward Albee

Frank D. Gilroy

Eugene Ionesco

AUGSBURG PUBLISHING HOUSE
MINNEAPOLIS, MINNESOTA

To my parents

for their encouragement in drama and in the gospel

CONTENTS

ACKNOWLEDGEMENTS

To Grove Press, Inc.

  for permission to quote an excerpt from *Inadmissible Evidence*, Copyright © 1965 by John Osborne Productions Ltd., and for permission to quote an excerpt from *Exit the King*, Copyright © 1963 by John Calder (Pub) Ltd.

To Random House, Inc.

  for permission to quote an excerpt from *The Subject Was Roses*, by Frank D. Gilroy, Copyright © 1965.

To The Viking Press, Inc.

  for permission to quote an excerpt from *After the Fall*, Copyright © 1964 by Arthur Miller, and for permission to publish an excerpt from *The Price*, Copyright © 1968 by Arthur Miller and Ingeborg M. Miller, Trustee.

To Atheneum Publishers, Inc.

  for permission to quote an excerpt from *A Delicate Balance*, by Edward Albee. Copyright © 1966 by Edward Albee.

PREFACE

Too often we are tempted to tune out what modern playwrights, novelists and filmmakers are saying to us. They treat ugly, depressing subjects and show ugly, depressing people. We are in different worlds, we think. We are "Christian" people. They don't have anything to say to us and, because of the kinds of things they do say—shocking, sordid, repugnant to our sensibilities— we shouldn't be listening to them.

Now, there are a couple of things wrong with that attitude. First of all, we *are* in the same world, like it or not. And, in the second place, many of these writers and artists are exposing, in a powerful way, the problems and sicknesses of this world and its people.

What, then, do we gain by listening?

I find it interesting that in his letter to Titus the apostle Paul quotes one of the "prophets" of Crete, where Titus was pastor, to help make a point: "One of themselves, a prophet of their own, said, 'Cretans are always liars, evil beasts, lazy gluttons.' This testimony is true.

Therefore rebuke them sharply, that they may be sound in the faith."

Similarly, can we not also quote the "prophets" of our contemporary society—playwrights, for example—to reinforce our witness to the world they represent? Serious writers are concerned about exposing the maladies which trouble people and which damage human relationships. We in the church want to do the same thing. The difficulty is that when we start our message about "sin" the man of the world shrugs it off and says, "Oh, you Christians are *supposed* to talk that way." But we can also say to him, "Look, this is how *your own prophets* see you and your world and the people around you . . . haunted by failure, disturbed inwardly by a feeling of guilt, driven by fears, caught up very often in a sense of futility, separated from your fellows, rebellious toward death. Life is meant to be different from this. Can we talk about it together?" This gives us an entrance into the thinking of men and women of the world through the message of their own prophets.

Next, through the work of a playwright who does his work honestly and compassionately, we can hear a cry of human need.

In Christian groups we have a habit of talking about sin in general. But how can we catch the conscience of a person and convict him of his guilt and need of forgiveness? How can we show him that God cares about him *as he is?* In order to be specific we must know what people are thinking and feeling inside themselves. The serious modern playwrights can help us because they grapple with human problems which they see to be real and immediate. Their observations must have a basis in truth, or they will not have people listening to them either! Many times, as Christians, we are talking past people. We say the religious words but we don't touch the heart's need. A playwright who has accurately probed the human condition can point us to such a need and help us relate to it in specific terms.

Finally, once we know some of the things that are bothering people, we can respond to a particular need more meaningfully with the good news from God. We can formulate a direct answer to a direct problem, speak a specific forgiveness to a specific sin, make God's love real in a real situation. For instance, modern man may be very vulnerable to the idea of "betrayal." He knows that he has been guilty of "selling out" other people all around him in order to get an advantage for himself. To converse with him about betrayal may "hit home" and convict him, and this will be followed by the assurance that God's love in Christ has forgiveness for such sins of betrayal also.

These writers are, at least partially, putting people under the law. Their emphasis is on people failing people. We must add the dimension of people failing God. Then we must apply the gospel of hope and comfort in Jesus Christ. The sermons following the play excerpts are an attempt to show how this may be done. They will serve best as examples or as material to be reworked and reshaped. Each preacher must decide how the message of the play segment may best be interpreted and applied to the people before him. Out of this study he will direct the gospel application more fully and extensively to the needs of the local situation.

—ROBERT HOWARD CLAUSEN

PRESENTING THE PLAYS

The play excerpts in this volume are intended to be used as preparation for the meditations within the framework of a worship service. There are a number of ways of doing this. These are some possibilities:

(1) The scenes may be staged realistically before the congregation. This requires full memorization of the lines and some effort to simulate the setting. Attention is given to costumes, makeup, and properties, and lighting, where possible, is used to accent the mood of the scene. This method of presentation demands the maximum work from the actors and the director.

(2) The scenes may be presented with appropriate movement by actors who have memorized the lines, but the theatrical accessories may be dispensed with or held to a minimum. There may be a suggestion of costume, a few essential properties and an intelligent use of available lighting,

but the main responsibility is placed on the actor and his personal resources.

(3) The presentations may be done in readers' theater style. The actors are usually seated with scripts in hand or with the scripts before them on reading stands. There are differing opinions as to whether readers' theater should be straight reading or whether the actor may look away from his script and use gestures, but both are done. This type of performance eliminates the need to memorize lines and avoids other production work.

(4) The actors, when doing the scenes, may be situated *behind* the congregation, as in the balcony, holding scripts as they read and interpret, audible but not seen. The result is like a radio drama. Because the people of the congregation cannot see the actors and the voices are coming from behind them, adequate projection must be assured and the importance of the vocal interpretation is heightened.

(5) The scenes may be taped in advance and presented over an amplification system. This may provide an advantage in a "controlled" performance, with sound effects and a uniformly good projection level.

Even a reading performance needs careful rehearsal; but with the above options, any church may select the style of presentation which is most advantageous in terms of the experience of the actors and the time available.

Some of the plays contain language which the playwright has felt necessary to be true to the character and the situation, but which is deemed inappropriate for a church setting. A judgment must be made at the production level as to how this problem will be solved. There must always be concern for the artistic integrity of the play. But there is little value in offending people with a word or a phrase to a point where they reject the whole experience. A deletion of the offensive language is a step which must be taken with proper concern for the whole surrounding dramatic structure. In some cases, the substitution of less offensive words may still sustain the desired effect.

1

The Cry of Failure

From

After the Fall

by

Arthur Miller

INTRODUCTION:

Arthur Miller is perhaps most widely known as the author of the play *Death of a Salesman,* phenomenally successful on the American and international stages, made into a distinguished motion picture, and later seen by millions on television.

Miller's play *After the Fall* sets before us a lawyer named Quentin who is recalling events and people in his life, and who is torn between hope and despair about his existence.

After the failure of one marriage, Quentin meets a young girl named Maggie whose openness and attractiveness appeal to him. They are married, but the happiness doesn't last for long. She becomes a successful entertainer, and suspicion and mistrust becloud their lives.

Maggie turns to drink and pills to deaden her feelings of depression. Quentin wants to leave her, and yet feels some responsibility for her.

We now listen to a conversation between Quentin and Maggie from Act Two of *After the Fall.* The setting is the bedroom. Maggie has a pill bottle in her hand.

AFTER THE FALL

QUENTIN: Maggie, you want to die and I don't know
any more how to prevent it. Maybe it was
just my being out in the real world for
twenty-four hours again, but it struck me
that I'm playing with your life out of some
idiotic hope of some kind that you're suddenly going to come out of this endless
spell. I think somebody ought to be with
you who has no illusions of that kind, and
simply watches constantly to prevent it.

MAGGIE: Maybe a little love would prevent it.

QUENTIN: But how would you know, Maggie? Not
that I love you, but if I did, would you
know any more? Do you know who I am?
Aside from my name? I'm all the evil in
the world, aren't I? All the betrayal, the
broken hopes, the murderous revenge?

MAGGIE: And how'd that happen? Takes two to
tango, kid.

15

With a sneer she opens the bottle. He stands at once.

QUENTIN: I'm not sitting here if you take any more. Especially on top of whisky; that's the way it happened the last time.

She spills out a few into her palm and he walks a step away.

Okay. Carrie's in her room; I've told her to look in here every few minutes, and if she sees signs she's to call the ambulance. Good night.

MAGGIE: She won't call the ambulance, she loves me.

QUENTIN: That's why she'll call the ambulance. Which is what I would have done last year if I'd loved you instead of loving myself. I'd have done it two years ago, in fact, but I didn't know what I know now.

MAGGIE: *Sneering.* What do you know now? You're spoiled. What do you know?

QUENTIN: A suicide kills two people, Maggie. That's what it's for. So I'm removing myself and perhaps it will lose its point.

She appears to consider for a moment;

then carefully takes two pills and swallows them.

Right.

He walks, determined, upstage. And when he is a far distance:

MAGGIE: *On a new level; softly, and without any antagonism:* What's Lazarus? *He halts, without turning back. She looks about for him, not knowing he has left.*

Quentin?

Not seeing him, she starts up off the bed; a certain alarm . . . Quen?
He comes halfway back.

QUENTIN: Jesus raised him from the dead. In the Bible. Go to sleep now.

MAGGIE: Wha's 'at suppose to prove?

QUENTIN: The power of faith.

MAGGIE: What about those who have no faith?

QUENTIN: They only have the will.

MAGGIE: But how do you get the will?

QUENTIN: You have faith.

MAGGIE: Some apples.

He smiles, turns again to go.

I want more cream puffs.

He turns back; doesn't answer.

And my birthday dress? If I'm good? Mama? I want my mother.

She sits up, looks about as in a dream, turns and sees him.

Why you standing there?

She gets out of bed, squinting, and comes up to him, peers into his face; her expression comes alive.

You . . . you want music?

QUENTIN: All right, you lie down, and I'll put a little music on.

MAGGIE: No, you; you, sit down. And take off your shoes. I mean just to rest. You don't have to do anything. *She goes to the machine, turns it on; jazz.* Was I sleeping?

QUENTIN: For a moment, I think.

MAGGIE: Was she . . . was anybody else here?

QUENTIN: No. Just me.

MAGGIE: Is there smoke?

QUENTIN: Your mother's dead and gone, dear, she can't hurt you any more, don't be afraid.

MAGGIE: *In a helpless voice of a child.* Where are you going to put me?

QUENTIN: *His chest threatening a cry.* Nowhere dear—he'll decide with you. He might be here tonight.

MAGGIE: See? I'll lay down. *She hurries to the bed, lies down.* See?

QUENTIN: Good.

MAGGIE: 'Member how used to talk to me till I went to sleep?

QUENTIN: Yes, dear. *He sits beside the bed.*

MAGGIE: *She struggles for lucidity, for some pose of quiet charm.* It nice in Chicago?

QUENTIN: Yes, very nice. *The caricature of pleasantry nearly shakes off the world.* Was it nice here?

MAGGIE: *She takes a strange, deep breath.* Ya.

Some birds came. And a mouse. You . . .
you could have the pills if you want.

QUENTIN: *Stands.* I'll have Carrie come in and get
them. *He starts to move.*

MAGGIE: *Clutching the bottle.* No. I won't give
them to Carrie.

QUENTIN: Why do you want me to have them?

MAGGIE: *Extending them.* Here.

QUENTIN: *Pause.* Do you see it, Maggie? Right now?
You're trying to make me the one who
does it to you? I take them; and then we
fight, and then I give them up, and you
take the death from me. You see what's
happening? You've been setting me up for
a murder. Do you see it? *He moves backward.* But now I'm going away; so you're
not my victim any more. It's just you, and
your hand.

MAGGIE: *Slowly retracting her hand, looking at it.*
But ask Ludwig—I only wanted to be
wonderful so you be proud, and you—

QUENTIN: And for yourself, dear, mostly for yourself. You were ambitious; it's no crime.

You would have been everything you are without me.

MAGGIE: *About to weep.* You ran out of patience, right?

QUENTIN: That's right. Yes.

MAGGIE: So you lied. Right?

QUENTIN: Yes, I lied. Every day. We are all separate people.

MAGGIE: You wanted a happy whore. Right?

QUENTIN: Not a whore, but happy, yes. I didn't want too much trouble.

MAGGIE: But Jesus must have loved her. Right?

QUENTIN: Who?

MAGGIE: Lazarus?

QUENTIN: *Pause; he sees, he gropes toward his vision:* That's right, yes! He . . . loved her enough to raise her from the dead. But he's God, see . . .

Felice appears, raising her arm in blessing.

. . . and God's power is love without limit. But when a man dares reach for that . . .

He has moved toward Felice, pursuing his truth.

he is only reaching for the power. Whoever goes to save another person with the lie of limitless love throws a shadow on the face of God. And God is what happened, God is what is; and whoever stands between another person and her truth is not a lover, he is . . .

He breaks off, lost, peering, and turns back to Maggie for his clue, and as Felice vanishes . . .

And then she said.

He goes back to Maggie, crying out to invoke her.

And then she said!

MAGGIE: *She is trying to wipe a film from before her thought.* But . . . but . . . will my father find me if you put me . . . No. I mean . . . what's moral?

QUENTIN: *In the tension of trying to recall.* To tell the truth.

MAGGIE: No-no . . . against yourself even.

QUENTIN: Yes.

MAGGIE: *She turns to him; her look is insane, and the truth is purified of all restraint.* Well? *A cry is gathering in her, as though only now did she know there was no return.* I hear you. Way inside. Quentin? My love? I hear you! Tell me what happened! *Her tears tell her sanity. He weeps facing her.*

QUENTIN: *On the verge of the abyss.* Maggie, we . . . used one another.

MAGGIE: *Weeping, calling.* Not me, not me!

QUENTIN: Yes, you. And I. "To live," we cried, and "Now," we cried. And loved each other's innocence as though to love enough what was not there would cover up what was. But there is an angel, and night and day he brings back to us exactly what we want to lose. And no chemical can kill him, no blindness dark enough to make him lose his way; so you must love him, he keeps truth in the world. You eat those pills like power, but only what you've done will save you. If you could only say, I have been cruel, this frightening room would open! If you could say, I have been kicked around, but I have been just as inexcusably vicious to others; I have called my husband idiot in public, I have been utterly selfish despite my generosity, I have been hurt by a long line of men but I have cooperated with my perse-cutors . . . .

MAGGIE: *She has been writhing, furious at this exorcism.* Son of a bitch!

QUENTIN: And I am full of hatred, I, Maggie, the sweet lover of all life—I hate the world!

MAGGIE: Get out of here!

QUENTIN: Hate women, hate men, hate all who will not grovel at my feet proclaiming my limitless love for ever and ever!

She spills a handful of pills into her palm. He speaks desperately, trying not to physically take the pills from her.

Throw them in the sea; throw death in

the sea and drink your life instead; your rotten, betrayed, hateful mockery of a life. That power is death, Maggie! Do the hardest thing of all—see your own hatred, and live!

Wretched man that I am! Who will deliver
me from this body of death? Thanks be to
God through Jesus Christ our Lord!

Romans 7:24-25

The Cross Means Hope

Arthur Miller, in his play *After the Fall,* reveals
the anguish of a man who discovers that his nature
and all of his actions are flawed, imperfect, poisoned
at the root. The very love he professes for others
often masks a selfishness and a desire to use these
people for his own ends.

The man Quentin, about whose life and past the
play revolves, sees this flaw, this imperfection, this
streak of evil not only in himself but as a corrosive
element in the character of all humanity. He thinks
about the monstrous sum of human suffering represented by the World War II extermination camps
in Germany, and he says:

"And I am not alone, and no man lives who would
not rather be the sole survivor of this place than all
its finest victims? What is the cure? Who can be

innocent again on this mountain of skulls? I tell you
what I know! My brothers died here . . . but my
brothers built this place; our hearts have cut these
stones! And what's the cure! *His family and friends
appear in the light.* No, not love. I loved them all,
all! And gave them willingly to failure and to death
that I might live, as they gave me and gave each
other, with a word, a look, a truth, a lie—and all in
love!"

None of us is innocent!

When the chips are down, he is saying, we give
up others, anyone, to save ourselves . . . and what
passes for love is a draining of others' lives to feed
our own.

During the course of action in the play, Quentin,
who is a lawyer, is representing a friend named Lou.
He'd rather not, because the case may damage his
personal reputation, but he does it out of friendship. Then he learns that Lou has killed himself by
jumping in front of a subway train. And Quentin
says, "When I saw him last week he said a dreadful
thing. I tried not to hear it. He said that I turned
out to be the only friend he had." Asked why that
was dreadful, Quentin responds: "It just was. I don't
know why. I didn't dare know why. But I dare now.
It was dreadful because I was not his friend either,
and he knew it. I'd have stuck it to the end, but I
hated the danger in it for myself, and he saw through
my faithfulness; and he was not telling me what a
friend I was, he was praying I would be—'Please be
my friend, Quentin,' is what he was saying to me, 'I

am drowning, throw me a rope!' . . . Because I
wanted out—and he saw it, and proved it in the joy
. . . the joy . . . the joy I felt now that my danger had
spilled out on the subway track!"

Thus, even what we do in the guise of love, of
friendship, of duty, is often unwillingly done. We
do it for appearance's sake or for society's approval,
but even as we are doing it we wish there were a
way out, and we rejoice if the necessity, the burden
is taken from us.

There is the flaw in our behavior, the imperfection, the hollowness at the center of things.

In the scene with Maggie, as we heard, Quentin
gets on the subject of God and says that "God's
power is love without limit. But when a man dares
reach for that, he is only reaching for the power."

In other words, when a person strives to be like
God he is not aspiring to possess that limitless love
because that means giving oneself for others. That
person is reaching out for the *power* which he thinks
will put him on top so that he can dominate and
use others for his own interests. There is nothing
godlike in man. It's all a lie.

And, what is worse, Arthur Miller says through
Quentin, we don't want to recognize the problem.
The flaw is in our nature but we don't want to
see it. Our actions are evil but we defend them,
justify them, and try to convince ourselves and others that they are good.

Quentin says to Maggie, "If you could only say,

I have been cruel, this frightening room would open! If you could say, I have been kicked around, but I have been just as inexcusably vicious to others; I have called my husband an idiot in public, I have been utterly selfish despite my generosity, I have been hurt by a long line of men but I have cooperated with my persecutors . . . "

But Maggie doesn't want to hear it. And Quentin confesses his own hypocrisy: "And I am full of hatred, I, Maggie, the sweet lover of life—I hate all who will not grovel at my feet, proclaiming my limitless love for ever and ever!"

To paraphrase Quentin's confession: I hate all who will not treat me as if I am God!

Now a Christian recognizes that what Arthur Miller is describing in this play is original sin—the inner corruption of man's will and nature, the bent toward evil and away from God, the stain that seeps through and discolors all our thoughts and words and actions, the inability to produce anything perfect and pure.

In Romans Chapter 7, the apostle Paul says the same thing that Quentin says in the play:

> "For I know that nothing good dwells within me, that is, in my flesh. I can will what is right, but I cannot do it. For I do not do the good I want, but the evil I do not want is what I do." (Verses 18-19)

Arthur Miller, by his title *After the Fall,* alludes to the dark chapter of Genesis 3, the rebellion of Adam and Eve against God, and the entrance of sin and its infection into the bloodstream of the human race. But more urgent than a backward look is the immediate problem. Quentin felt it. The apostle Paul expresses it:

> "For I delight in the law of God, in my innermost self, but I see in my members another law at war with the law of my mind and making me captive to the law of sin which dwells in my members. Wretched man that I am! Who will deliver me from this body of death?" (Romans 7:21-24)

In my body is sin, imperfection, conflict, death! Where do I find help?

The apostle Paul points to it in his next words: "Thanks be to God through Jesus Christ our Lord!"

How is Jesus Christ the answer to this anguish of human failure, to this vision of ourselves which is often too bitter to face?

First of all, he delivers us from the condemnation of our sins, from the judgment we face at the hands of a righteous God (that is, a God who is absolutely right in everything he does).

The good news of the Bible is precisely this, that "there is therefore now no condemnation for those who are in Christ Jesus . . . Sending his own Son in the likeness of sinful flesh and for sin, he [God] condemned sin in the flesh." (Romans 8:1, 3) As true, perfect, representative man, Christ bore our sins and God condemned our sins in Christ. For the sake of Christ God pardons us and declares us to be in a restored fellowship with him.

Secondly, the Bible offers hope of a change from imperfection to perfection.

In Jesus Christ we see God's "love without limit" focused in a person who was flesh and blood as we are. But in him there is no flaw, no imperfection, no sin . . . only perfect obedience to the Father and a complete outgoing love toward people.

God wants to form the character of Jesus in us.

He not only forgives our sins, but, as we walk by faith in his Word, he puts his Spirit into us to free us from the domination of our sin impulses, to purge our character from sin's infection, to unclog the inner channels of our nature, and to let the love of Christ flood through our being. It's a process that begins here, but ends in heaven. It is still a time of struggle. But a new power is available within us . . . the power of God which, if we draw upon it by faith and activate it by a steady use of God's Word, will enable us to rise above the downward pull of sin and to demonstrate in some measure and with increasing effectiveness that limitless love of God.

But we have to start in honesty.

We have to start with confession.

We can't pretend that the problem isn't in us.

"Do the hardest thing of all," said Quentin to Maggie—"See your own hatred, and live!"

2

The Cry of Guilt

From

Inadmissible Evidence

by

John Osborne

INTRODUCTION:

John Osborne, the English playwright, leaped into fame with his play *Look Back in Anger*. His play *Luther* has won much acclaim and has aroused much controversy with its treatment of the great Reformer.

In *Inadmissible Evidence* a thirty-nine year old London lawyer, Bill Maitland, is on trial, in the courtroom of his mind, for what he has made of his life. As he looks back over his existence, his offenses rise to condemn him.

The Law Society is about to take action against him for his unethical practices, and, during the play his fellow-workers leave him, one by one. His telephonist, Joy, is the last to go.

The only person remaining with Maitland is his mistress, Liz, who has come to visit him at his office. In this scene there are references to Anna and Jane, Bill's wife and daughter, from whom he is estranged.

The office girl, Joy, has just left. Let us listen now to this conversation between Liz and Bill.

INADMISSIBLE EVIDENCE

LIZ: My darling: are you all right?

BILL: Splendid.

LIZ: Why don't you come home?

BILL: Yes.

LIZ: I'm sorry, I had to come. You didn't answer the telephone.

BILL: Didn't I?

LIZ: I wasn't interrupting anything was I?

BILL: No.

LIZ: Oh, come along. I don't know why you don't admit you knock off that girl—

BILL: Because I don't need to.

35

LIZ: I keep giving you opportunities.

BILL: Well, I don't want them. I don't want to be cued in by you—

LIZ: It's a lot to ask, you know.

BILL: Yes, I see that too.

Pause.

LIZ: You do ask a great deal of both of us, you know. It's unnecessary and it diminishes you.

BILL: True.

LIZ: I do love you.

BILL: Your assessment's impeccable. As usual.

LIZ: You're a dishonest little creep.

BILL: Why the "little"? Because you seem to have more authority than I have? *Pause.* You're not *bigger*. You're cleverer. More accomplished, more generous. And more loving.

LIZ: I've always managed to avoid guilt. It's a real peasant's pleasure, you know. For people without a sliver of self-knowledge or courage.

BILL: There *are* other qualities besides courage.

LIZ: Well?

BILL: Cowardice for instance. For example.

LIZ: I've not seen you since Thursday. I thought somehow we'd manage to resolve the pain of that particular evening. Even on the telephone.

BILL: So did I. So we did. Till the next time.

LIZ: I love you so dearly. I can't think what to say to you.

BILL: I think you will.

LIZ: Why can't you trust me? Please?

BILL: It isn't easy.

LIZ: I know.

BILL: It isn't easy to trust someone: you're busily betraying. Sit down. I can't see you over there. I don't like my clients sitting half way across the room talking to themselves.

She sits. Pause.

LIZ: What do you want me to do?

BILL: Do?

LIZ: Yes, my darling . . . do.

BILL: I don't know. I haven't given it much thought.

LIZ: Did you see Jane?

BILL: Yes.

LIZ: How was that?
He looks at her.
I see. So. What's going to happen?

BILL: Liz!

LIZ: What?

BILL: I'm tired of being watched. I'm tired of being watched by you, and observed and scrutinized and assessed and guessed about.

LIZ: Who gives a damn!

BILL: You do, you did. But you won't.

LIZ: What are you saying? Do you want me to go—? Really?

BILL: Well, you're the one who insisted on what you called an ethic of frankness.

LIZ: Believe me, the last thing I would insist on is an ethic like that. I can't think of anything more destructive.

Phone rings.

BILL: Hullo . . . No, everyone's gone.

LIZ: Well, we know who that is.

BILL: I'm just clearing up . . . I told you, everyone's gone. . . . Just me. . . . Yes, she *is* here. . . . Because I couldn't be bothered to tell the truth. . . . Listen, now's not a very good time, is it? Look, I'll ring you back.

Pause. Liz looks slightly mocking, but doesn't exploit it. She is too concerned for him.

When I leave you sometimes and I get in, deliberately, of course, about three or four A.M. and Anna's lying there in bed, pretending to be asleep. After making love to you and the drive back, I'm so tired and there's the following morning a couple of hours away only, but I pretend to sleep because I can't to begin with. We both just lie there. And if I'm lucky or drunk enough and I do go to sleep, she lies there choking in silence unable to sleep again till she wakes me in the morning. Do you know I can't remember one detail of what she looks like, not since I left this morning and we'd had the row about the weekend. I sat down to read the Charterhouse of Parma while you were away at Christmas. You said I'd like it. So I started. It took me ten days and I gave up round about the middle somewhere. I can't tell you what's it's about. I can't grasp anything. I used to be good at my job because I had what they called an instinct and a quick brain. Quick! I can't get through the Law reports. I leave everything to Hudson and now he's gone, and I wouldn't leave a camel's breakfast to Jones even if he *were* still here.

Liz: Bill. What are we going to do?

Bill: Go away. I suppose.

Liz: But where?

Bill: Far away, as far away as possible from this place. There's no place for me here.

Liz: *Half humoring.* I never think of you as a traveller.

Bill: Meaning?

Liz: Well, you never seem to enjoy it much, do you? *Pause.* Well, do you?

Bill: Damn it, I've, I've travelled thousands of miles in the past few years for various clients in the last—

Liz: Oh yes, flights to New York and Amsterdam and Geneva. They're just business men's bus rides.

Bill: What do you want then? What should I be? Lady Hester Stanhope with a briefcase of legal documents perched on a camel?

Liz: I just don't think of your business trips as travel—

Bill: Oh, travel—

Liz: They're just for getting from one place to another for a particular purpose.

Bill: *Bitterly.* Well, what do *you* call travelling?

Liz: Well, like, like going in a boat around the Isles of Greece.

Bill: Yes. With a lot of tight-lipped, fast-shooting dons on the look out for someone else's wife or crumpet.

LIZ: When you're anywhere, you're always desperately miserable. You want to get back.

BILL: Yes?

LIZ: Oh, to your clients. Or something. I was thinking, on my way here, and now . . .

BILL: Well?

LIZ: I was thinking: perhaps you'd rather I didn't come away for the weekend.

Silence. He faces her.

I just thought you seemed . . . as if . . . you might . . . want to be alone.

Pause.

BILL: I was only waiting, from the moment you came in, for you to say that.

LIZ: I'm sorry to be so predictable. One often is, you know, when someone knows you well and loves you.

BILL: As I do. As I certainly do.

LIZ: I was trying my hardest to be honest. It's a failing—

BILL: Well, why don't you take something for it.

LIZ: I don't care what you are or what you do—

BILL: Or who I am.

LIZ: I need you.

BILL: Not that word, please.

LIZ: You pretend to be ill and ignorant just so you can escape reproach. You beggar and belittle yourself just to get out of the game.

BILL: Whenever I do it, I enjoy, I think you do know, being some, some sort of, sort of good and comfort and pleasure to you because I love you. I don't love you for the sake of that pleasure. I can get it anywhere.

She touches his shoulder and kisses the back of his head. He won't look up.

LIZ: You can always ring me.

BILL: But you won't be there.

Deliver me from bloodguiltiness, O God, thou God of my salvation, and my tongue will sing aloud of thy deliverance.

Psalm 51:14

The Cross Means Forgiveness

In John Osborne's play *Inadmissible Evidence,* Bill Maitland, the central character, is in a situation where people are cutting him off.

At the very beginning of the play he comes into his office late and says, "I couldn't get a taxi. That's the first time I've never got one . . . I don't know what they're doing."

His office clerk, Shirley, gives him notice and walks off the job.

He goes to a party with his wife, Anna, and says about her friends, "I just felt everyone was cutting me . . . cutting me . . ."

Of one of his clients he says, "I scared her off. In some way. I could feel her withdrawing from me."

Of a fellow lawyer he says, "I just rung up old

44

Winters. You know . . . Well, he wouldn't speak to me."

Of his father, he says, "My old father lives in the country, as you know, but he doesn't want to see me these days."

To his daughter Jane he says, "They're all pretending to ignore me. No they're not pretending, they are! And that'll be the going of you, except that it's happened already."

His telephonist, Joy, walks out on him, his partner, Hudson, goes to work for somebody else, and, as we heard, in the final scene of the play his mistress, Liz, leaves him.

In his closing speech, Maitland phones his wife and says, "Do you think I should come home? . . . I don't think there's much point, do you?"

At the end of the play he is deserted, alone, waiting.

And the strange thing throughout the play is that Maitland is not surprised at these things. It's as if he *expected* them. As if it is all a judgment upon him.

For, as the play sets it up, Bill Maitland is on trial. His whole life is on trial . . . in his own mind.

He must account for what he has said, for how he has acted, for what he has done to people.

And he knows his guilt.

He has used people, he has exploited people, he has betrayed people, and always he has acted to serve his own selfish ends, to gratify his own desires.

He talks about love, but it is not true love, giving itself for the happiness of others. In a flash of honesty at the beginning of the play he says, "with . . . love, I succeeded, I succeeded in inflicting, quite certainly inflicting, more pain than pleasure."

He has betrayed his wife by rejecting her and by being unfaithful to her . . . "She lies there choking in silence."

He betrays his daughter by showing no fatherly interest or sympathy: "Do you want to get rid of me? Do you? Because I want to get rid of you."

He betrays his fellow-workers because he is jealous of their character or their abilities.

He betrays his clients' trust by seeing his crimes in their problems and so, justifying himself, begins to accuse them.

He betrays his profession by indulging in dishonest, shabby practices.

He even betrays his mistress with the women in his office.

And when people leave him, drop him, cut him off, he recognizes this as an exposure of his own guilt.

As Walter Kerr wrote in the *New York Herald-Tribune:* "The crowding dark is upon Mr. Osborne's hero, but it is a dark he is inventing for himself . . . In the jarring twilight he is his own accuser, his own jailer, his own judge, and . . . he sees that . . . he is guilty."

What does the cross say in answer to this cry of human need—the problem of human guilt?

First of all, the cross underscores the *reality* of human guilt.

And, what is more, it says that everyone is implicated.

In the words of Romans 3:23, "All have sinned and fall short of the glory of God."

Now, there may be a variation in the degree, but not in the nature of our crime.

We may not all be Bill Maitlands; but not one of us has loved each other as we should.

Or, putting it another way: our guilt is just this, that we have not been to other people everything that we should be!

Wife to husband . . . husband to wife.

Parent to child . . . child to parent.

Neighbor to neighbor.

In each of our histories there are times when we have used people, exploited people, betrayed people, in order to advance our own interests.

Or we have *failed* people by not giving ourselves to them in answer to some need because we felt it was demanding too much and would cost us something more than at that moment we were willing to pay.

There is one aspect of guilt which the play doesn't bring out sharply.

That is, that when we are betraying people we are at the same time betraying God.

He created us in his image.
He created us to love as he loves.
He created us to care as he cares.
He created us to give as he gives.
When we fail one another, we fail him.
We betray his trust.
We betray one another, and are separated from one another.

We betray God, and we are separated from God.

Guilt . . . loneliness . . . waiting for the end with increasing despair. That's how the play ends.

But the cross makes another answer possible.

It says that something amazing and awesome happened there.

It says that Jesus Christ the perfect Son of God assumed our guilt and paid its penalty. All of our betrayals and all of our failures were heaped on him, and he bore them in his own body on the cross.

It says that "God was in Christ reconciling the world to himself, not counting their trespasses against them" (2 Corinthians 5:19) . . . that is, God treats us as if we have no guilt because Christ suffered for our sins, the just for the unjust.

He who knew no sin was made sin for us that we might be made the righteousness—the perfect rightness—of God in him.

To believe that is to have forgiveness, peace with God, and the beginning of new relationships with God and with our fellowmen.

But we must begin with confession.

We must say, "I am guilty."

We must say, "Deliver me from bloodguiltiness, O God, thou God of my salvation."

God will hear and honor that cry from an anguished heart when it is directed to him through Jesus Christ.

He will forgive, he will make clean.

But something follows—

"My tongue will sing aloud of thy deliverance."

There will be a change in our language, in our attitudes, in our actions, in our whole way of life if we are living in praise of God who delivers us from the gnawing inner anguish of sin and failure and betrayal.

We will see fellow human beings not as objects to be used, abused and misused, but as individuals whose worth and dignity is to be respected, whose true personhood is to be protected and nurtured, whose lives should be better and happier for touching ours, and who, hopefully, will see the reality of Christ and his love as it is revealed in what we are and in what we do.

3

The Cry of Fear

From

A Delicate Balance

by

Edward Albee

INTRODUCTION:

After attracting attention with a series of short plays, Edward Albee became firmly established as one of America's leading playwrights with his full-length play *Who's Afraid of Virginia Woolf?*, a searing treatment of a marriage disintegrating through mutual contempt and hate. His next major stage work was *Tiny Alice*, and then came *A Delicate Balance*.

In this last-named play, we meet a middle-aged couple, Agnes and Tobias, awaiting the return home of their daughter, Julia, whose fourth marriage has just broken up. With them in their home is Claire, Agnes's sister, an alcoholic.

Before Julia arrives, there is the sound of a car in the drive, then a knock on the door. Agnes opens it and finds that Harry and Edna, very close friends, have come to see them.

Let's listen to this conversation from Act One of *A Delicate Balance*.

A DELICATE BALANCE

There is a knock at the door, Agnes answers it.

AGNES: Edna? Harry? What a surprise, Tobias, it's Harry and Edna. Come in. Why don't you take off your . . .

Harry and Edna enter. They seem somewhat ill at ease, strained for such close friends.

TOBIAS: Edna!

EDNA: Hello, Tobias.

HARRY: *Rubbing his hands; attempt at being bluff.* Well, now!

TOBIAS: Harry!

CLAIRE: *Too much surprise.* Edna! *Imitates Harry's gruff voice.* Hello, there, Harry.

53

EDNA: Hello, dear Claire! *A little timid.* Hello, Agnes.

HARRY: *Somewhat distant.* Evening . . . Claire.

AGNES: *Jumping in, just as a tiny silence commences.* Sit down. We were just having a cordial . . .

Curiously loud. Have you been . . . out? Uh, to the club?

HARRY: *Is he ignoring Agnes' question?* I like this room.

AGNES: To the club?

CLAIRE: *Exaggerated, but not unkind.* How's the old Harry?

HARRY: *Self-pity entering.* Pretty well, Claire, not as good as I'd like, but . . .

EDNA: Harry's been having his shortness of breath again.

HARRY: *Generally.* I can't breathe sometimes . . . for just a bit.

TOBIAS: *Joining them all.* Well, two sets of tennis, you know.

EDNA: *As if she can't remember something.* What have you done to the room, Agnes?

AGNES: *Looks around with a little apprehension, then relief.* Oh, the summer things are off.

EDNA: Of course.

AGNES: *Persisting in it, a strained smile.* Have you been to the club?

HARRY: *To Tobias.* I was talking to Edna 'bout having our books done in leather; bound.

TOBIAS: Oh? Yes?

Brief silence.

CLAIRE: The question—'less I'm going deaf from all this alcohol—was *Southern accent* "Have you-all been to the club?"

AGNES: *Nervous, apologetic covering.* I wondered!

HARRY: *Hesitant.* Why . . . no, no.

EDNA: *Ibid.* Why, why, no, Agnes . . .

AGNES: I wondered, for I thought perhaps you'd dropped by here on your way from there.

HARRY: . . . no, no . . .

AGNES: . . . or perhaps that we were having a party, and I'd lost a day . . .

HARRY: No, we were . . . just sitting home.

EDNA: *Some condolence.* Agnes.

HARRY: *Looking at his hands.* Just . . . sitting home.

AGNES: *Cheerful, but lack of anything better to say.* Well.

TOBIAS: Glad you're here. Party or not!

HARRY: *Relieved.* Good to see you, Tobias!

EDNA: *All smiles.* How is Julia?

CLAIRE: Wrong question. *Lifts her glass.* May I have some brandy, Tobias?

AGNES: *A savage look at Claire, back to Edna.* She's coming home . . . I'm afraid.

EDNA: *Disappointment.* Oh . . . not again!

TOBIAS: *Getting Claire's glass, attempted levity.* Just can't keep that one married, I guess.

EDNA: Oh, Agnes, what a shame!

HARRY: *More embarrassed than sorry.* Gee that's too bad.

Silence.

CLAIRE: Why *did* you come?

AGNES: Please! Claire! *Back, reassuring.* We're *glad* you're here. We're glad you came to surprise us.

TOBIAS: *Quickly.* Yes!

Harry and Edna exchange glances.

HARRY: *Quite sad and curious about it.* We were . . . sitting home . . . just sitting home . . .

EDNA: Yes.

AGNES: *Mildly reproving.* We're *glad* to *see* you.

CLAIRE: *Eyes narrowing.* What happened, Harry?

AGNES: *Sharp.* Claire! Please!

TOBIAS: *Wincing a little, shaking his head.* Claire . . .

EDNA: *Reassuring him.* It's all right, Tobias.

AGNES: I don't see why people have to be questioned when they've come for a friendly . . .

CLAIRE: *Small victory.* Harry wants to tell you, Sis.

EDNA: Harry?

HARRY: We . . . well, we were sitting home . . .

TOBIAS: Can I get you a drink, Harry?

HARRY: *Shakes his head.* . . . I . . . we thought about going to the club, but . . . it's, it's so crowded on a Friday night . . .

EDNA: *Small voice, helpful, quiet.* . . . with the canasta party, and getting ready for the dance tomorrow . . .

HARRY: . . . we didn't want to do that, and I've . . . been tired. And we didn't want to do that . . .

EDNA: . . . Harry's been tired this whole week.

HARRY: . . . so we had dinner home, and thought we'd stay . . .

EDNA: . . . rest.

AGNES: Of course.

CLAIRE: Shhh.

AGNES: *Rather vicious.* I will not SHHH!

HARRY: Please?

Waits a moment.

TOBIAS: *Kind.* Go on, Harry.

HARRY: So we were sitting, and Edna was doing that—that panel she works on . . .

EDNA: *Wistful, some loss* . . . my needlepoint . . .

HARRY: . . . and I was reading my French; I've got it pretty good now—not the accent, but the . . . the words.

A brief silence.

CLAIRE: *Quietly.* And then?

HARRY: *Looks over to her, a little dreamlike, as if he didn't know where he was.* Hmm?

CLAIRE: *Nicely.* And then?

HARRY: *Looks at Edna.* I . . . I don't know quite what happened then; we . . . we were . . . it was all very quiet, and we were all alone . . .

Edna begins to weep, quietly; Agnes notices, the others do not; Agnes does nothing.

. . . and then . . . nothing happened, but . . .

Edna is crying more openly now.

. . . nothing at all happened, but . . .

EDNA: *Open weeping; loud.* WE GOT . . . FRIGHTENED.

Open sobbing; no one moves.

HARRY: *Quiet wonder; confusion.* We got scared.

EDNA: *Through her sobbing.* WE WERE . . . FRIGHTENED.

HARRY: There was nothing . . . but we were very scared.

Agnes comforts Edna, who is in free sobbing anguish; Claire lies slowly back on the floor.

EDNA: We . . . were . . . terrified.

HARRY: We were scared.

Silence; Agnes comforting Edna, Harry stock still. Quite innocent, almost childlike. It was like being lost: very young again, with the dark, and lost. There was no . . . thing . . . to be . . . frightened of, but . . .

EDNA: *Tears; quiet hysteria.* WE WERE FRIGHT-
ENED ... AND THERE WAS NOTHING.

Silence in the room.

HARRY: *Matter-of-fact, but a hint of daring under it.*
We couldn't stay there, and so we came here.
You're our very best friends.

EDNA: *Crying softly now.* In the whole world.

AGNES: *Comforting, arms around her.* Now, now,
Edna.

HARRY: *Apologizing some.* We couldn't go anywhere
else, so we came here.

AGNES: *A deep breath, control.* Well, we'll . . . you
did the right thing . . . of course.

TOBIAS: Sure.

EDNA: Can I go to bed now? Please?

AGNES: *Pause; then, not quite understanding.* Bed?

HARRY: We can't go back there.

EDNA: Please?

AGNES: *Distant.* Bed?

EDNA: I'm so . . . tired.

HARRY: You're our best friends in the world. Tobias?

TOBIAS: *A little bewilderment; rote.* Of course we are, Harry.

EDNA: *On her feet, moving.* Please?

Cries a little again.

AGNES: *A million things going through her head, seeping through management.* Of . . . of course you can. There's . . . there's Julia's room, and . . . *Arm around Edna.* Come with me, dear.

Reaches doorway; turns to Tobias; a question that has no answer.

Tobias?

HARRY: *Rises, begins to follow Edna, rather automaton-like.* Edna?

TOBIAS: *Confused.* Harry?

HARRY: *Shaking his head.* There was no one else we could go to.

Exits after Agnes and Edna. Claire sits up, watches Tobias, as he stands for a moment, looking at the floor; silence.

CLAIRE: *A small, sad chuckle.* I was wondering when
 it would begin . . . when it would start.

TOBIAS: *Hearing her only after a moment.* Start?

 Louder.

 START?

 Pause.

 WHAT?!

CLAIRE: *Raises her glass to him.* Don't you know yet?

 Small chuckle.

 You will.

The Lord is my light and my salvation;
whom shall I fear?

Psalm 27:1

The Cross Means Security

Have you ever been in a situation where, suddenly, for no apparent reason, you felt afraid?

You didn't know what it was, where it was, why it was, but you felt watched, threatened, endangered?

If you have ever had that experience, you will identify with the feelings of Edna and Harry in this scene from Edward Albee's play *A Delicate Balance*.

To a person who has never had that kind of experience, the whole happening will seem very strange.

A middle-aged couple—intelligent, prosperous, respectable—are sitting in their comfortable home, the wife doing needlepoint, the husband studying French, when, suddenly, as they put it:

"We got frightened . . . scared . . . terrified. . . .
It was like being lost: very young again, with the

dark, and lost. There was no . . . thing . . . to be frightened of, but . . . WE WERE FRIGHTENED, AND THERE WAS NOTHING . . ."

The play never really explains why they were frightened.

Albee uses words as dark symbols, and you must guess what they represent.

But certainly the mood of the scene is unmistakable—fear, entering into and gripping two people to a point where they can't stay at home alone, but must go and seek company at the home of their friends.

Albee's play does suggest people living in a spiritual vacuum . . . their lives are confused, aimless, drifting.

They are floundering, looking for answers, unable to give them to one another.

May we not attach this meaning to the scene, that when our lives are empty of faith and hope, fears of all kinds will crowd in to upset us, to torment us, to haunt us?

There was an emptiness in the lives of Harry and Edna which seemed to invite fear.

Are there not also times when fear tries to take us over?

It may be fear about our health, about our job, about our future.

It may be a nameless, undefined fear that something terrible is happening in our world, something which threatens our homes, our families, our society, our country, all that life has meant to us and means to us, and that we are helpless before it.

It may be the fear of death in its suddenness, its finality, its irresistable power.

When fear strikes, it can be chilling and terrible.

Now, when fear attacks us, two things can happen: either we will be overwhelmed by fear, as were Harry and Edna, or we can repel the fear.

Once again we look to the cross and find that it has an answer to this cry of human need.

The cross confronts us with the person of Jesus Christ.

Jesus claimed to be God, to speak as God, to act as God.

Thus, what happened at the cross, if we believe Jesus, is God's action.

The Bible interprets this as a love action.

God saw man adrift on a sea of sin, of fear, of death.

The sin in us keeps fighting God, keeps telling us that we know better than God, keeps pushing us away from God.

But instead of harmony our sinful actions create discord, frustration, hurt, and pain.

We don't have all the answers.

We fail other people, we fail God, we fail ourselves.

And to all of this there is a penalty attached. The wages of sin is death.

Something within us dies when we turn from God and try to live independent of him.

Our actions make us enemies of God's holy purposes, and we find ourselves under wrath, condemnation and judgment.

God in Christ deals with this problem.

He sent his perfect Son to live in this imperfect world in order to demonstrate perfect love and to call men back to God's way.

But first a barrier had to be broken down . . . the barrier of human sin, waywardness and rebellion.

What about the penalty which holiness must exact?

Jesus Christ, God the Son, that perfect man, became sin for us and felt the wrath, the condemnation, the judgment of God.

He bore our sins in his own body on the cross.

God looks at us through the cross and says, "I have dealt with your sins. The penalty is paid. Justice is answered. Peace is restored."

To believe that word, to trust it, to live by it, is to know the forgiveness and friendship of God.

What does this have to do with fear?

The cross tells us that at the heart of the universe is a God of love who cares for us and who has given supremely of himself to free us from the curse of sin and death and to reunite us with himself in an eternal, living relationship. If God cared for us in that great need, he will care for us in our other needs also.

Perhaps the closest thing to an interpretation of Harry and Edna's fear in the play is when one of the characters asks, "Harry and Edna: what do they want?" . . . Another replies: "Succor, pardon?, comfort, warmth. A special room with a light, or the door ajar so you can look down the hall from the bed and see that Mommy's door is open."

Must we see this only as a weakness? Are we not all children of the heavenly Father?

Do not we also, deep down in our inmost being, want help, pardon, comfort, warmth?

And, taking off from the human picture which Albee gives, does not the cross set the door of heaven ajar for us? . . . May we not look through it and to it and past it and see that God's door is open to us?

"For God has not destined us for wrath, but to obtain salvation through our Lord Jesus Christ, who died for us so that whether we wake or sleep we might live with him." (1 Thessalonians 5:10)

It is dishonest and foolish to say that we do not have fears. God doesn't ask that hypocrisy.

Let's admit our fears, face them, and then repel them before they can overwhelm us.

Let's take comfort from the promise of the Scriptures that nothing exists which can separate us from the love of God in Jesus Christ.

We can release our fears to God.

Let's say, "There are a lot of things in life that want to make me afraid, but they won't beat me down. I'll face life trusting that nothing is bigger than God, and God's love and God's power. He will let nothing defeat his plan for me. He will let nothing do a lasting hurt to me."

"The Lord is my light and my salvation; whom shall I fear?"

At the end of *A Delicate Balance*, Agnes says, after Harry and Edna have left:

> "What I find most astonishing, I think, is the wonder of the daylight, the sun. All the centuries, milleniums—all the history—I wonder if that's why we sleep at night, because the darkness still . . . frightens us? They say we sleep to let the demons out—to let the mind go raving mad, our dreams and nightmares, all our logic gone awry, the dark side of reason. And when the daylight comes again . . . comes order with it."

The Christian need not fear the night, nor darkness, nor death, nor demons, nor any other thing.

If our lives are securely God's in Christ, the God who neither slumbers nor sleeps will have us in his constant care. And at the end of the world's night will come the great day of the Lord—the day when perfect order is restored.

Until then, with the Psalmist we will say, not with fear but with confidence: "In peace I will both lie down and sleep; for thou alone, O Lord, makest me dwell in safety." (Psalm 4:8)

4

The Cry of Futility

From

The Price

by

Arthur Miller

INTRODUCTION:

In his play *The Price* Arthur Miller presents two brothers, Walter, a surgeon, and Victor, a policeman, brought together after many years of separation.

Their father has recently died, and their mother had died previously, so they must now dispose of their parents' property.

The setting of the play is New York, in the family house which is soon to be demolished. Stacked everywhere is a clutter of furniture which is to be sold to a second-hand dealer.

As the two brothers carry on their conversation, one becomes aware that each has made a decision in the past as to what he would do with his life, and, in the intervening time, has paid a price for that decision.

Victor, the policeman, is in the scene with his wife, Esther, and Walter, the surgeon, is the first to speak as we listen to this conversation from Act Two.

THE PRICE

WALTER: . . . Actually, I've been trying to call you for quite some time now.

VICTOR: What for?

WALTER: *Suddenly, with a strange, quick laugh, he reaches and touches Victor's knee.*

Don't be suspicious!

VICTOR: *Grinning.* I'm just trying to figure it out, Walter.

WALTER: Yes, good. All right. *Slight pause.* I thought it was time we got to know one another. That's all.

Slight pause.

VICTOR: You know, Walter, I tried to call you a couple of times before this about the furniture—must be three years ago.

73

WALTER: I was sick.

VICTOR: *Surprised.* Oh . . . Because I left a lot of messages.

WALTER: I was quite sick. I was hospitalized.

ESTHER: What happened?

WALTER: *Slight pause. As though he were not quite sure whether to say it.* I broke down.

Slight pause.

VICTOR: I had no idea.

WALTER: Actually, I'm only beginning to catch up with things. I was out of commission for nearly three years. *With a thrust of success:* But I'm almost thankful for it now —I've never been happier!

ESTHER: You seem altogether different!

WALTER: I think I am, Esther. I live differently, I think differently. All I have now is a small apartment. And I got rid of the nursing homes—

VICTOR: What nursing homes?

WALTER: *With a removed self-amusement.* Oh, I

owned three nursing homes. There's big money in the aged, you know. Helpless, desperate children, trying to dump their parents—nothing like it. I even pulled out of the market. Fifty per cent of my time now is in City hospitals. And I tell you, I'm alive. For the first time. I do medicine, and that's it. *Attempting an intimate grin:* Not that I don't soak the rich occasionally, but only enough to live, really.

It is as though this was his mission here, and he waits for Victor's comment.

VICTOR: Well, that must be great.

WALTER: *Seizing on this minute encouragement.* Vic, I wish we could talk for weeks, there's so much I want to tell you. . . . *It is not rolling quite the way he would wish and he must pick examples of his new feelings out of the air.* I never had friends —you probably know that. But I do now. I have good friends. *He moves, sitting nearer Victor, his enthusiasm flowing.* It all happens so gradually. You start out wanting to be the best, and there's no question that you do need a certain fanaticism; there's so much to know and so little time. Until you've eliminated everything extraneous—*he smiles*—including people. And of course the time comes when you realize that you haven't merely been specializing in something—something has been specializing in you. You become a kind of instrument, an instrument that cuts money out of people, or fame out of the world. And it finally makes you stupid. Power can do that. You get to think that because you can frighten people they love you. Even that you love them.—And the whole thing comes down to fear. One night I find myself in the middle of my living room, dead drunk with a knife in my hand, getting ready to kill my wife.

ESTHER: Good Lord!

WALTER: Oh ya—and I nearly made it too! *He laughs.* But there's one virtue in going nuts—provided you survive, of course. You get to see the terror—not the screaming kind, but the slow, daily fear you call ambition, and cautiousness, and piling up the money. And really, what I wanted to tell you for some time now—is that you helped me to understand that in myself.

VICTOR: Me?

WALTER: Yes. *He grins warmly, embarrassed.* Because of what you did. I could never understand it, Vic—after all, you *were* the better student. And to stay with a job like that through all those years seemed . . . *He breaks off momentarily, the uncertainty of Victor's reception widening his smile.* You see, it never dawned on me till I got sick—that you'd made a choice.

VICTOR: A choice, how?

WALTER: You wanted a real life. And that's an expensive thing; it costs. *He has found his theme now; sees he has at last touched something in Victor. A breath of confidence comes through now.* I know I may sound terribly naive, but I'm still used to talking about anything that matters. Frankly, I didn't answer your calls this week because I was afraid. I've struggled so long for a concept of myself and I'm not sure I can make it believable to you. But I'd like to. *He sees permission to go on in Victor's perplexed eyes:* You see, I got to a certain point where . . . I dreaded my own work; I finally couldn't cut. There are times, as you know, when if you leave someone alone he might live a year or two; while if you go in you might kill him. And the decision is often . . . not quite, but almost . . . arbitrary. But the odds are acceptable, provided you think the right thoughts. Or don't think at all, which I managed to do till then. *Slight pause. He is no longer smiling; instead, a near embarrassment is on him.* I ran into a cluster of misjudgments. It can happen, but it never had to me, not one on top of the other. And they had one thing in common; they'd all been diagnosed by other men as inoperable. And quite suddenly the . . . the whole prospect of my own motives opened up. Why had I taken risks that very competent men had declined? And the quick answer, of course, is—to pull off the impossible. Shame the competition. But suddenly I saw something else. And it was terror. In dead center, directing my brains, my hands, my ambition—for thirty years.

Slight pause.

VICTOR: Terror of what?

Pause.

WALTER: *His gaze on Victor now.* Of it ever happening to me—*he glances at the center chair*—as it happened to him. Overnight, for no reason, to find yourself degraded and thrown-down. *With the faintest hint of impatience and challenge:* You know what I'm talking about, don't you?

Victor turns away slightly, refusing commitment.

Isn't that why you turned your back on it all?

VICTOR: *Sensing the relevancy to himself now.* Partly. Not altogether, though.

WALTER: Vic, we were both running from the same thing. I thought I wanted to be tops, but what it was was untouchable. I ended in a swamp of success and bankbooks, you on civil service. The difference is that you haven't hurt other people to defend yourself. And I've learned to respect that, Vic; you simply tried to make yourself useful.

ESTHER: That's wonderful—to come to such an understanding with yourself.

WALTER: Esther, it's a strange thing; in the hospital, for the first time since we were boys, I began to feel . . . like a brother. In the sense that we shared something. *To Victor:* And I feel I would know how to be friends now.

The wise man's path leads upward to life,
that he may avoid Sheol beneath.

Proverbs 15:24

The Cross Means Dedication

Of the two brothers in Arthur Miller's play *The Price,* Walter is the one who, in the eyes of the world, would appear to be a success. He was a surgeon who made big money; he had a big name and a big reputation. Yet, in this conversation with his brother, Walter looks at his life and admits that something had been missing.

He acknowledges that he had been aiming at the wrong goals, living by the wrong standards, and making the wrong judgments, as a result of which he "broke down" and was "out of commission" for three years.

In Proverbs 15:24 we read, "The wise man's path leads upward to life, that he may avoid Sheol beneath."

In the Old Testament, the word Sheol refers variously to death, to the grave, to hell. By failing to take the path which leads upward to life one is, in effect, choosing the way of death.

There is a twofold warning here. It is possible for us to make wrong decisions about life which can create a hell already on this earth. But more than this, and more terribly, such wrong decisions can destroy our opportunity for happiness in the world to come.

In *The Price*, what was it that had put Walter on the way which led downward to death?

Walter describes the source of his problem in a number of ways.

He says that in a fanatic determination to be the best you eliminate "everything extraneous—including people."

He says, "You become a kind of instrument, an instrument that cuts money out of people, or fame out of the world."

He talks about "the slow daily fear you call ambition . . . and piling up the money."

He talks about the deception of power: "You get to think that because you can frighten people they love you."

He talks about the fear of losing your status—"to find yourself degraded and thrown down."

He says, "I thought I wanted to be tops, but what it was was untouchable. I ended in a swamp of success and bankbooks."

He admits that he has "hurt other people" to defend himself, what he is, and what he considers to be his own.

It adds up to a life governed by the ambition to get things for oneself, rather than to do things for others.

His actions were controlled by a desire for power, status, success, reputation, and money.

He found himself using people to get what he wanted, and then fighting them off because he felt that they threatened what he had.

But the end of it was not happiness but emptiness, dissatisfaction, a sense of futility.

The *Chicago Daily News* once ran a series of articles about young, self-made millionaires. It told about one man who had made his millions and become a great success in the commercial world, but who had lost his wife and children along the way under the pressure of the drive for the top. "If I could start over," he said, "I wouldn't do it again."

Emptiness . . . Futility . . . Dissatisfaction . . . because people have not found the path that "leads upward to life."

What is this path that leads to life?

First of all, it's found in Christ Jesus.

In the great Good Shepherd Chapter, John 10, Jesus says, "The thief comes only to steal and kill and destroy; I came that they may have life, and have it abundantly" (v. 10)

Jesus wants to give us a full, complete, satisfying life, beginning here and now.

In the second place, a key condition to our entering upon this path is our willingness to serve others just as Jesus served us.

In Matthew 20:25-28 he says:

"You know that the rulers of the people have power over them, and their leaders rule over them. This, however, is not the way it shall be among you. If one of you wants to be great, he must be the servant of the rest; and if one of you wants to be first, he must be your slave—like the Son of Man, who did not come to be served, but to serve, and to give his life to redeem many people." (TEV)

This is the answer which the cross gives to the cry of emptiness and futility in human life.

"I wanted to be tops," said Walter.

"If you want to be tops where it really counts," says Jesus, "in my kingdom, you can't cut money out of people, frighten people with your power, or hurt other people to defend your own interests or your position of superiority. You've got to learn to serve people."

Jesus didn't just talk like this.

He acted this out.

He served people.

He responded to their needs, their hungers, their feelings.

He used his power not to exalt himself but to lift others to physical health, to spiritual peace, to a better knowledge of God, of themselves, and of the path which "leads upward to life."

Finally, and supremely, Jesus served by giving his life to redeem many.

He served us by taking our sins upon himself—also our sins of self-centered ambition and our use of people to serve our own ends—in order that he might deliver us from sin's curse, which is physical death, spiritual death, eternal separation from God.

> His life, his all, he gave
> When he was crucified;
> Our burdened souls to save,
> What fearful death he died!
> But each of us, though dead in sin,
> Through him eternal life may win.

To believe in that word, in that Christ, in that cross and what it stands for is to know forgiveness, inner peace, and fellowship with God.

But to identify yourself with that Christ and with that cross is, at the same time, to commit yourself to the way of service.

The Bible says, "In love, serve one another." (Galatians 5:13)

Husbands and wives, are you just "living" with each other, or are you concerned about serving each other?

Do you serve one another by being attentive to one another's needs, by giving to each other needed love, affection, patience, understanding, encouragement, and support?

Parents, are you talking with your children or at them, regarding them or disregarding them, listening to them or turning them off? Are you so absorbed in your needs that you forget they have needs, too?

Children, is your behavior demanding, selfish, inconsiderate? Do you think most of the time about what you want, do you demand things for your happiness? Do you take time to think about your parents' needs, how you can serve them and bring them happiness?

All of us must analyze our situation:

What goals am I aiming at?

What standards am I living by?

What measurements am I using for success in life?

We can be ruthless, calculating, determined to succeed for ourselves alone.

We can take and take and take for ourselves.

But the Bible says, "But if you bite and devour one another take heed that you are not consumed by one another." (Galatians 5:15)

That way is the path that leads downward to death.

"The wise man's path leads upward to life."

It's the path opened to us by God, the way set forth in the person, the life, the death, the resurrection of Jesus Christ.

It's the way of repentance, of faith, of submission to God.

It's the way of giving oneself to serving God and other people.

Walter said, after beginning to serve others, "I tell you, I'm alive."

You can say that, too, when you take the path which leads upward to life, the path that begins at the cross of Jesus Christ.

5

The Cry of Estrangement

From

The Subject Was Roses

by

Frank D. Gilroy

INTRODUCTION:

Frank D. Gilroy was a television and film writer with one well-received off-Broadway play, *Who'll Save the Plowboy?*, when he became an instant success as a Broadway playwright with the production of *The Subject Was Roses* in 1964.

It is May, 1946, and in their West Bronx, New York, apartment, John Cleary, 50, and his wife, Nettie, are celebrating their son Timmy's discharge from the army and return home at the end of World War II.

Neither John nor his wife want to admit it openly, but their marriage is holding together by the frailest of threads. Each is hoping that Timmy's return and presence in the home will supply the necessary something which will change things for the better. But it doesn't work.

As the play unfolds, tensions between John and Nettie flash into open conflict, and Timmy gets into arguments with his father about religion, money and family affairs. In the heat of anger the father even strikes the son.

At the end of the play, Timmy resolves to leave. His father, John, tries to persuade him to stay.

Let us listen in now to this conversation between father and son, from Act Two of *The Subject Was Roses*.

THE SUBJECT WAS ROSES

TIMMY: Good morning.

JOHN: Morning.

TIMMY: Mother said you wanted to see me.

JOHN: Sleep well?

TIMMY: Yes.

JOHN: Good . . .

TIMMY: You wanted to see me?

JOHN: Mother says you're leaving.

TIMMY: Yes.

JOHN: Rather sudden, isn't it?

TIMMY: Not really.

JOHN: Mind telling me why?

TIMMY: I just think it's best.

JOHN: For who?

TIMMY: Everyone.

JOHN: Crap! *(Timmy starts from the room.)* Wait. *(The note of entreaty in his voice causes Timmy to halt.)* I didn't mean that. . . . The fact is I don't blame you for wanting to leave. I had no business hitting you.

TIMMY: That's not why I'm going.

JOHN: If there was any way I could undo last night, I would.

TIMMY: It's not a question of last night.

JOHN: If I had it to do over again I'd cut my arm off.

TIMMY: Pop, listen—

JOHN: I don't know what gets into me sometimes.

TIMMY: Pop! *(John looks at him.)* I'm not leaving

because of anything that happened last night . . . I always intended to leave.

JOHN: You never mentioned it.

TIMMY: I planned to stay a couple of weeks and then go.

JOHN: A couple of days isn't a couple of weeks.

TIMMY: It's not like I'm going to China.

JOHN: Why two days instead of two weeks?

TIMMY: Because I know that if I stay two weeks I'll *never* leave.

JOHN: If it's what I said yesterday, about me being the boss and you'd have to do what I said—forget it.

TIMMY: It's not that.

JOHN: I was just letting off steam.

TIMMY: *It's not that.*

JOHN: As far as I'm concerned you're a man—you can come and go as you please, do as

you please. That goes for religion, drinking, anything.

TIMMY: How can I make you understand?

JOHN: Even girls. I know how it is to be your age.
Give me a little advance notice and I'll see
that you have the house to yourself whenever you want.

TIMMY: Pop, for Chrisake.

JOHN: *(Flares momentarily.)* What kind of language is that? *(Then hastily:)* I'm sorry. I
didn't mean that. Talk any way you want.

TIMMY: I don't know what to say to you.

JOHN: What I said yesterday about the Jews, I
was just trying to get a rise out of you.

TIMMY: I know.

JOHN: The time those bums from St. Matthew's
jumped the I-cash-clothes man. I was the
one who saved him.

TIMMY: I know.

JOHN: Whole crowd of people watching but I
was the only one who did anything.

TIMMY: Do you think I could forget that?

JOHN: Stay another week. Just a week.

TIMMY: I can't.

JOHN: Stay till Wednesday.

TIMMY: No.

JOHN: Do you have any idea how your mother looked forward to your coming home?

TIMMY: Yes.

JOHN: Then how can you do it?

TIMMY: We're just going around in circles.

JOHN: What happens to the lake house?

TIMMY: What do you mean?

JOHN: Without you, what's the good of it?

TIMMY: I'll be spending time there.

JOHN: I thought we'd have a real summer together like before the war.

TIMMY: You're making this a lot tougher than it has to be.

JOHN: *Did you expect me to say nothing? Like her? . . .*

TIMMY: Are you through?

JOHN: *(Trying a new tack.)* I know what the trouble is. You know what the trouble is? You're like me . . . Stubborn . . . All the Clearys are stubborn . . . Would rather die than admit a mistake . . . Is that a fact? Yes or no?

TIMMY: I don't know.

JOHN: *(Points to himself.)* Well, here's one donkey who's seen the light. I've been wrong in my dealings with you and I admit it.

TIMMY: Pop!

JOHN: Not just wrong last night, but all along. Well, those days are gone forever, and I'll prove it. . . . You know how much money I have?

TIMMY: I don't want to know.

JOHN: Fourteen thousand three hundred and fifty-seven dollars.

TIMMY: Pop!

JOHN: Plus a bit more in stocks . . . Now *you* admit that *you* made a mistake—admit you don't really want to leave and we'll forget the whole thing.

TIMMY: I *don't* want to leave.

JOHN: See—

TIMMY: But I'm leaving.

JOHN: *(Turning away.) Then go and good riddance!*

TIMMY: Listen to me.

JOHN: The sooner the better.

TIMMY: *Listen to me! (Pauses—then goes on quietly, intensely.)* There was a dream I used to have about you and I. . . . It was always the same. . . . I'd be told that you were dead and I'd run crying into the street. . . .

Someone would stop me and ask why I was crying and I'd say, "My father's dead and he never said he loved me."

JOHN: *(Trying unsuccessfully to shut out Timmy's words.)* I only tried to make you stay for her sake.

TIMMY: I had that dream again last night. . . . Was thinking about it this morning when something occurred to me that I'd never thought of before.

JOHN: She's the one who'll miss you.

TIMMY: It's true you've never said you love me. But it's also true that I've never said those words to you.

JOHN: I don't know what you're talking about.

TIMMY: I say them now—

JOHN: *I don't know what you're talking about.*

TIMMY: I love you, Pop. *(John's eyes squeeze shut, his entire body stiffens, as he fights to repress what he feels.)* I love you.

(For another moment, John continues his losing battle, then, overwhelmed, turns, extends his arms. Timmy goes to him. Both in tears, they embrace.)

Through him [Jesus] then let us continually offer up a sacrifice of praise to God, that is, the fruit of lips that acknowledge his name. Do not neglect to do good and to share what you have for such sacrifices are pleasing to God.

Hebrews 13:15-16

The Cross Means Reconciliation

In Frank Gilroy's play *The Subject Was Roses,* Timmy comes home after three years of service in the Army during World War II. He comes back to his parents, John and Nettie, whom he wants to love. But something keeps getting in the way.

Each of his parents wants to love him and to have a good relationship with him. But something keeps getting in the way.

The two parents try to present themselves to their son as if things are going all right between them. But sometimes keeps getting in the way.

And at the end of the play Timmy decides to leave home, feeling that he has to make a new start for himself somewhere, alone.

What was wrong?

As the play develops, Timmy recalls that his father's past ill behavior of drinking, staying away from home, and causing grief and heartache to his mother, had created a miserable atmosphere in his childhood:

> At one point in the play, he says to his father: "All those nights I lay in bed waiting for your key to turn in the door. Part of me praying you'd come home safe, part of me dreading the sound of that key because I knew there'd be a fight. . . . All those mornings I woke up sick. Had to miss school. The boy's delicate, everyone said, has a weak constitution. . . . From the day I left this house I was never sick. Not once. Took me a long time to see the connection."

Timmy knows that his mother's rejection of his father is the result of many unhappy and difficult experiences. But Timmy comes to see his mother's faults also.

As a boy he had been sorry for his mother and sided with her against his father. He says to her, "That's what we must seem like to him—an alliance. Always two against one. Always us against him . . ."

He says to his mother, "You said you've never understood him." And Nettie says, "And never will." But Timmy continues, "Have you ever really tried? . . . Have you ever tried to see things from his point of view?" . . . And he suggests that the father did many of the things that he did because the mother never did communicate to her husband some sympathy and understanding for *his* wants and desires.

But in the closing scene of the play, just before he leaves home, Timmy implicates himself also. He tells his father of a dream he frequently had, where he would run crying into the street . . . "Someone would stop me and ask me why I was crying, and I'd say, 'My father's dead, and he never said he loved me.' . . . I had that dream again last night . . . Was thinking about it this morning when something occurred to me that I'd never thought of before. It's true you've never said you love me. But it's also true that I never said those words to you."

The right kind of communication had been lacking between husband and wife, between father and son. There was no communication of love, of affection, of sympathy, of understanding of the other person's needs.

And there can be no closeness, no unity, no togetherness unless there is free, open, constructive communication between people.

The Bible says in Hebrews 13:15 and 16:

"Through him [Jesus] then let us continually offer up a sacrifice of praise to God, that is, the fruit of lips that acknowledge his name. Do not neglect to do good and to share what you have for such sacrifices are pleasing to God."

The meaning of the word *communicate* is linked with sharing.

God has not failed to communicate with us.

His "I love you" is written large over the cross of Jesus Christ.

Jesus came as the living expression of God the Father's love for us sinners. "In this is love, not that we loved God but that he loved us and sent his Son to be the expiation for our sins." (1 John 4:10)

The wrath of God against sin and sinners was directed at his own Son who represented all sinners before the judgment seat of God.

On the cross, in the anguish of his soul, Jesus felt sin's curse, sin's penalty, sin's separation from the righteous Father.

God says, "I love you . . . you, sinner, and you and you . . ."

He says it at the cross, and he repeats it in each baptism, each preaching of the good news of forgiveness through faith in Jesus Christ, each Holy Communion meal.

Now, we need to communicate with God.

We need to offer our "sacrifice of praise . . . the fruit of lips that acknowledge his name."

Our neglect of prayer, of worship, of Holy Communion means that we are breaking off communication with God.

We are putting a distance between ourselves and God when we fail to use these opportunities to communicate effectively to God our "I love you . . . I love you, God, because you first loved me."

But, more than this, the text reminds us, we are

not to "neglect to do good and to share what you have."

This involves communication with other people.

We may blame the other person, criticize the other person, reject the other person because we feel that he—or she—is failing us.

The factors which effect a breakdown in human relationships are indeed many and complex.

But should we not also look to ourselves?

And as we examine our actions, our conduct, our communication, may we not often have cause to say with Timmy, "I never said those words to you"?

Affections can grow cold, marriages can fall apart, love can die when a human heart, starved emotionally, fails to hear the words it wants to hear: "I love you."

But along with words we need to communicate love by "doing good": by helping one another, by serving one another, by being patient with one another, by being sensitive enough to act before one has to be told to act; by doing extra things, kind things, unexpected things which signal to the other person, unmistakably, "I love you."

We do good by putting ourselves in another's place, by seeing things from the other person's point of view, by responding with alertness to needs we see arising in others.

How about it husbands?

How about it wives?

How about it fathers?

How about it mothers?

How about it sons?

How about it daughters?

Are you sharing what you have, beginning with yourself?

Are you saying, "I love you"?

Are you showing "I love you" by doing good to and for one another?

And you see, the text tells us that God looks upon this as an expression of our thanksgiving to him.

Doing good in love to one another is an offering to God and he is as well-pleased with this as he is with our prayers and praise.

We would never have known the fulness of God's love if he hadn't spoken it through Jesus Christ and shown it at the cross. The other person won't know our love unless we say it and show it.

The cross meets our need of wanting to be loved by telling us—and showing us—that God loves us. It helps to overcome the tragic human problems of separation and estrangement by reminding us to communicate our love meaningfully to other people.

Timmy finally got it out.

He said, "I love you, Pop. I love you."

Let's be sure we're communicating this love—in our marriages and in our homes; and, after that, to the world outside.

6

The Cry of Death

From

Exit the King

by

Eugene Ionesco

INTRODUCTION:

Eugene Ionesco is a native of Rumania who has been a French citizen since 1938.

In company with Samuel Beckett and other writers Ionesco launched the Theatre of the Absurd in the 1950's, and his plays have depicted human existence as, by turns, grotesque, fantastic, and bitterly comic.

Ionesco's play *Exit the King* retains some of these characteristics but, while extremely imaginative in its language and setting, its central situation is intensely and recognizably human.

At the very beginning of the play King Berenger is told that he will die by the time the play ends. As the play progresses, we see him age, his physical powers weaken, and his kingdom and power shrivel to nothingness.

Through it all Berenger rebels powerfully, pitifully and pathetically against the fact of death and the extinction of his existence.

With the king are his first queen, Marquerite, plain and practical; his second queen, Marie, beautiful and romantic; Juliette, a nurse; the Doctor, who is also the Executioner; and the Guard.

Let us listen now as King Berenger begins the speaking in this scene from *Exit the King*. The setting is a room in Berenger's palace.

EXIT THE KING

KING: When I've gone, when I've gone.
          They'll laugh and stuff themselves silly
          and dance on my tomb. As if I'd never
          existed. Oh, please make them all re-
          member me! Make them weep and
          despair and perpetuate my memory in
          all their history books. Make everyone
          learn my life by heart. Make them all
          live it again. Let the school children
          and the scholars study nothing else but
          me, my kingdom and my exploits. Let
          them burn all the other books, de-
          stroy all the statues and set mine up
          in all the public squares. My portrait
          in every Ministry, my photograph in
          every office of every Town Hall, in-
          cluding Rates and Taxes, and in *all* the
          hospitals. Let every car and pushcart,
          flying ship and steamplane be named
          after me. Make them forget all other
          captains and kings, poets, tenors and
          philosophers, and fill every conscious

mind with memories of me. Let them learn to read by spelling out my name: B, E, BE for Berenger. Let my likeness be on all the ikons, me on the millions of crosses in all our churches. Make them say Mass for me and let *me* be the Host. Let all the windows light up in the shape and color of my eyes. And the rivers trace my profile on the plains! Let them cry my name throughout eternity, and beg me and implore me.

MARIE: Perhaps you'll come back again?

KING: Perhaps I will come back. Let them preserve my body in some palace, on a throne, and let them bring me food. Let musicians play for me and virgins grovel at my ice-cold feet.

                The King has risen in order to make this speech.

JULIETTE: *To Marguerite.* He is raving, Ma'am.

GUARD: *Announcing.* His Majesty the King is delirious.

MARGUERITE: Not yet. There's too much sense in

what he says. Too much, and not
enough.

DOCTOR: *To the King.* If such be your will, your
Majesty, we will embalm your body
and preserve it.

JULIETTE: As long as we can.

KING: Horror! I don't want to be embalmed.
I want nothing to do with that corpse.
I don't want to be burnt. I don't want
to be buried, I don't want to be thrown
to the wild beasts or the vultures. I
want to feel arms around me, warm
arms, cool arms, soft arms, strong
arms.

JULIETTE: He's not too sure what he *does* want.

MARGUERITE: We'll make up his mind for him. *To
Marie.* Now don't faint!

Juliette is weeping.

And there's another one! They're always the same!

KING: If I *am* remembered, I wonder for
how long? Let them remember me to
the end of time. And beyond the end

of time, in twenty thousand years, in two hundred and fifty-five thousand million years. . . . There'll be no one left to think of anyone then. They'll forget before that. Selfish, the lot of them. They only think of their own little lives, of their own skins. Not of *mine*. If the whole earth's going to wear out or melt away, it will. If every universe is going to explode, explode it will. It's all the same whether it's tomorrow or in countless centuries to come. What's got to finish one day is finished now.

MARGUERITE: Everything is yesterday.

JULIETTE: Even "today" will be "yesterday."

DOCTOR: All things pass into the past.

MARIE: My darling King, there is no past, there is no future. Remember, there's only a present that goes right on to the end, everything is present. Be present, be the present!

KING: Alas! I'm only present in the past.

MARIE: No, you're not.

MARGUERITE: That's right, Berenger, try and get things straight.

MARIE: Yes, my King, get things straight, my darling! Stop torturing yourself! "Exit" and "die" are just words, figments of our imagination. Once you realize that, nothing can touch you. Just be an eternal question mark: what . . . ? why . . . ? how . . . ? And remember: that you can't find the answers is an answer in itself. It's you, all the life in you, straining to break out. Dive into an endless maze of wonder and surprise, then you too will have no end, and can exist forever. Everything is strange and undefinable. Let it dazzle and confound you! Tear your prison bars aside and batter down the walls! Escape from definitions and you will breathe again!

DOCTOR: He's choking!

MARGUERITE: Fear cramps his vision.

MARIE: Open the floodgates of joy and light to dazzle and confound you. Illuminating waves of joy will fill your veins with wonder. If you want them to.

JULIETTE: You bet he does.

MARIE: *In a tone of supplication.* I implore you to remember that morning in June we spent together by the sea, when happiness raced through you and inflamed you. You knew then what joy meant: rich, changeless and undying. If you knew it once, you can know it now. You found that fiery radiance within you. If it *was* there *once*, it is *still* there *now*. Find it again. Look for it, in yourself.

KING: I don't understand.

MARIE: You don't understand anymore.

MARGUERITE: He never did understand himself.

MARIE: Pull yourself together!

KING: How do I manage that? No one can or will help me. And *I* can't help myself. Oh help me, sun! Sun, chase away the shadows and hold back the night! Sun, sun, illumine every tomb, shine into every hole and corner, every nook and cranny! Creep deep inside me! Ah! Now my feet are turning cold. Come and warm me, pierce my body, steal beneath my skin and blaze into my eyes! Restore their failing light, and let me see, see, see! Sun, sun, will you miss me? Good little sun, protect me! And if you're in need of some small sacrifice, then parch and wither up the world. Let every human creature die provided *I* can live forever, even alone in a limitless desert. I'll come to terms with solitude, I'll keep alive the memory of others, and I'll miss them quite sincerely. But I can live in the void, in a vast and airy wasteland. It's better to miss one's friends than to be missed oneself. Besides, one never is. Light of our days, come and save me!

DOCTOR: *To Marie.* This is not the light *you* meant.

MARGUERITE: *To Marie, or referring to Marie.* Love's labors lost. You're on the wrong track.

KING: Let me go on living century after century, even with a raging toothache. But I fear what must end one day has ended now.

MARGUERITE: It's only his speeches that are never

ending! *Indicating Marie and Juliette.* And these two weeping women. They only push him deeper in the mire, trap him, bind him and hold him up.

KING: No, there's not enough weeping, not enough lamentation. Not enough anguish. *To Marguerite.* Don't stop them weeping and wailing and pitying their King, their young King, old King, poor little King. *I* feel pity when I think how they'll miss me, never see me again, and be left behind all alone. I'm still the one who thinks about others, about everyone. All the rest of you, be me, come inside me, come beneath my skin. I'm dying, you hear, I'm trying to tell you. I'm dying, but I can't express it, unless I talk like a book and make literature of it.

DOCTOR: And that's the way it goes, to the bitter end. As long as we live we turn everything into literature.

MARIE: If only it could console him!

GUARD: *Announcing.* The King finds some consolation in literature!

KING:

No, no. I know, nothing can console me. It just wells up inside me, then drains away. Oh dear, oh dear, oh dear, oh dear, oh dear! *Lamentations—then without declamation, he goes on moaning gently to himself.* Help me, you countless thousands who died before me! Tell me how you managed to accept death and die. Then teach me! Let your example be a consolation to me, let me lean on you like crutches, like a brother's arms. Help me to cross the threshold you have crossed! Come back from the other side a while and help me! Assist me, you who were frightened and did not want to go! What was it like? Who held you up? Who dragged you there, who pushed you? Were you afraid to the very end? And you who were strong and courageous, who accepted death with indifference and serenity, teach me your indifference and serenity, teach me resignation.

The following dialog should be spoken and acted as though it were ritual, with solemnity, almost chanted, accompanied by various movements, with the actors kneeling, holding out their arms, etc.

JULIETTE: You statues, you dark or shining phantoms, ancients and shades . . .

MARIE: Teach him serenity.

GUARD: Teach him indifference.

DOCTOR: Teach him resignation.

MARGUERITE: Make him see reason and set his mind at rest.

KING: You suicides, teach me how to feel disgust for life! Teach me lassitude! What drug must I take for that?

DOCTOR: I could prescribe euphoric pills or tranquilizers.

MARGUERITE: He'd vomit them up!

JULIETTE: You remembrances . . .

GUARD: You pictures of days gone by . . .

JULIETTE: . . . which no longer exist but in our memories of memories . . .

GUARD: Recollections of recollections . . .

MARGUERITE: He's got to learn how to let go and then surrender completely.

GUARD: . . . we invoke you.

MARIE: You morning mists and dews . . .

JULIETTE: You evening smoke and clouds . . .

MARIE: You saints, you wise and foolish virgins, help him! For *I* cannot.

JULIETTE: Help him!

KING: You who died blissfully, who looked death in the face, who remained conscious of your end. . . .

JULIETTE: Help him!

MARIE: Help him all of you, help him, I beg you!

KING: You who died happy, what face did you see close to yours? What smile gave you ease and made *you* smile? What were the last rays of light that brushed your face?

JULIETTE: Help him, you thousand millions of the dead!

GUARD: Oh you, great Nothing, help the King!

KING: Thousands and millions of the dead.
                They multiply my anguish. I am the
                dying agony of all. My death is mani-
                fold. So many worlds will flicker out
                in me.

MARGUERITE: Life is exile.

KING: I know, I know.

DOCTOR: In short, Majesty, you will return to
                your own country.

MARIE: You'll go back where you came from
                when you were born. Don't be so
                frightened, you're sure to find some-
                thing familiar there.

MARIE: Other world, lost world, buried and
                forgotten world, rise again from the
                deep!

JULIETTE: Other plains, other valleys, other moun-
                tain chains . . .

MARIE: Remind them of your name.

MARGUERITE: Plunge into your memories, dive

through the gaps in your memory into a world beyond memory. *To the Doctor. This* is the only world he really misses!

MARIE:

Memories immemorial, appear before him! Help him!

KING:

When faced with death, even a little ant puts up a fight. Suddenly, he's all alone, torn from his companions. In him, too, the universe flickers out. It's not natural to die, because no one ever wants to. I want to exist.

JULIETTE:

That's all he knows. He wants to exist forever.

If a man die, shall he live again?

Job 14:14

The Cross Means New Life

In *Exit the King,* when King Berenger gets the news that he must die, he says, "I'm frightened."

He thinks "perhaps it's a nightmare."

He hopes for that "one chance in a thousand" by which he may escape death.

At the very least he wants to live on in people's memories, but then he realizes that when the whole universe is dead "there'll be no one left to think of anyone."

He's willing to accept life under any conditions, "even with a raging toothache."

He'll sacrifice anyone and everyone to have life for himself, for he says, "Let every human creature die provided I can live forever."

He gets little comfort from his second queen,

Marie, who says "exit" and "die" are just words . . . "figments of our imagination."

The Doctor can offer only pills and tranquilizers.

In desperation the King says, "Help me, you countless thousands who died before me. Tell me how you managed to accept death and die."

His first queen, Marguerite, says, "Plunge into your memories," but there is no help, and the King says, "It's not natural to die, because no one ever wants to die. I want to exist."

And Juliette the nurse says, "That's all he knows. He wants to exist forever."

All of the king's rebelling against the fact of death does no good. At the end of the play he is stripped of all his kingly accessories and left alone on stage to fade into nothingness.

The King is a representative Everyman.

And the play, *Exit the King*, is an eloquent expression of one of mankind's basic needs: to exist forever.

Job of old raised the cry in the Old Testament, forming the question which lies deep within each of our hearts: "If a man die, shall he live again?"

Or is death the end . . . nothingness . . . annihilation?

What is the answer of the cross to this cry of human need?

First of all, the Bible affirms the King's statement "It's not natural to die," in the sense that death is an intruder into God's creation. Man was created to live, not die. But man sinned, and sin opened the door to death. Physical death tells man generation after generation that he is a sinner, separated from God, and therefore dead spiritually.

Secondly, the Bible reveals that man cannot reverse the death process or evade it by his own efforts. According to Psalm 49:7-9:

> "Truly no man can ransom himself,
>   or give to God the price of his life,
>   ... that he should continue to live on forever."

What then is the answer?

"If a man die, shall he live again?"

We come to the third biblical truth, which is that God does provide an answer to this basic human need through the cross of Jesus Christ.

In order to deal with death, God had to deal with sin, the cause of death. This God has done in Jesus.

For this reason the Bible says in Hebrews 2:9:

> "But we see Jesus, who for a little while was made lower than the angels, crowned with glory and honor because of the suffering of death; so that by the grace of God he might taste death for everyone."

Christ was made to be sin for us and felt the sharp edge of God's judgment, the isolation from the righteous Father, but he was our substitute also in this that he tasted for each one of us the death that is sin's ultimate disgrace. He took our sin upon himself and paid its full penalty.

Why did Jesus, the Son of God, become man?

Why did he assume our flesh and blood?

Why did he go the way of the cross?

The Bible answers: "That through death he might destroy him who has the power of death, that is, the devil, and deliver all those who through fear of death were subject to lifelong bondage." (Hebrews 2:14-15)

To be a sinner, guilty before God and liable to sin's penalty, is to be in bondage to the devil, our tempter and accuser.

But Jesus Christ has paid the extreme penalty of sin for us.

Through him God forgives us our sins, declares us to be his friends, offers us a fresh beginning, and puts into us his life.

To trust that word of God is to possess its blessing: deliverance from the bondage of sin and death.

"For the wages of sin is death," declares Paul, "but the free gift of God is eternal life in Christ Jesus our Lord." (Romans 6:23)

Though death seemed to be the victor at the cross, its sting was pulled, its poison was drained, its power was cancelled.

It can no longer *hold us in bondage* because Jesus Christ has tasted death for us and has broken its bands. His resurrection from the dead shows that he is the stronger, and gives authority to his words, "I am the resurrection and the life; he who believes in me, though he die, yet shall he live, and whoever lives and believes in me shall never die." (John 11:25-26)

"If a man die, shall he live again?"

Job provided his own magnificent answer: "For I know that my Redeemer lives, and at last he will stand upon the earth; and after my skin has been thus destroyed, then from my flesh I shall see God, whom I shall see on my side, and my eyes shall behold, and not another." (Job 19:25-27)

At one point in *Exit the King*, Berenger bemoans his death, saying, "I never had time to get to know life."

Marguerite the Queen says, "Yet he had the greatest experts to tell him all about it. Theologians, people of experience, and books he never read."

The King says, "I never had time. I never had time. I never had time!"

Have you taken time to hear what the greatest expert of all in matters of life and death tells you? Jesus Christ the Son of God? He who became man for your sake? Who has suffered and died for your sins? Who has tasted death for you, but who rose from the grave to be revealed as the Son of God with power, and who says to you: "For this is the will of my Father, that every one who sees the Son and believes in him should have eternal life; and I will raise him up at the last day." (John 6:40)

Will you dare to face God and say, "I never had the time?"

God is giving you the time, now, to receive his Son, Jesus Christ, as your Lord and Savior, to put your heart's trust in him, and to accept through him God's gift of forgiveness and eternal life.

Gardner-Webb University

M. CHRISTOPHER WHITE
SCHOOL OF DIVINITY

*From the Library
of
Dr. Robert H. Culpepper*